Mindful of my Feelings

This book belongs to:

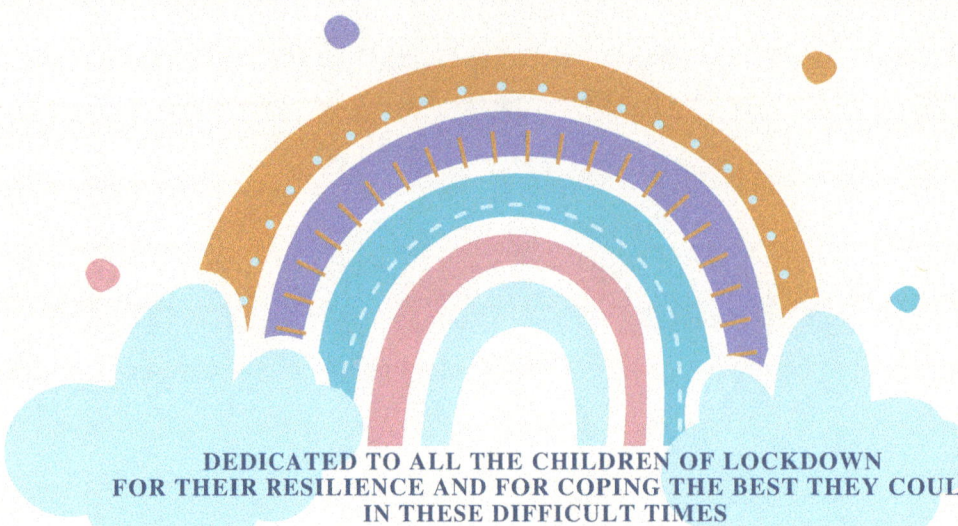

DEDICATED TO ALL THE CHILDREN OF LOCKDOWN
FOR THEIR RESILIENCE AND FOR COPING THE BEST THEY COULD
IN THESE DIFFICULT TIMES

A SPECIAL THANK YOU TO THREE AMAZING GIRLS:
EMILIA, EVIE AND RUBY
THEY WERE A GREAT HELP IN CREATING THIS BOOK

MINDFUL OF MY FEELINGS
COPYRIGHT © DOROTA PERKINS, 2021

FIRST EDITION: NOVEMBER 2021

AUTHOR
DOROTA PERKINS

COPY EDITOR
CAITLIN OWEN

CONTENT EDITOR
REBECCA SMITH

DESIGN AND LAYOUT
DOROTA PERKINS

ALL RIGHTS RESERVED.
NO PART OF THIS BOOK MAY BE REPRODUCED IN ANY FORM OR BY
AN ELECTRONIC OR MECHANICAL MEANS, INCLUDING INFORMATION STORAGE AND
RETRIEVAL SYSTEMS, WITHOUT PERMISSION IN WRITING FROM THE PUBLISHER,
EXCEPT BY A REVIEWER WHO MAY QUOTE BRIEF PASSAGES IN A REVIEW.

ISBN (PAPERBACK): 978-1-7398472-2-7

FURTHER INFORMATION ABOUT THIS BOOK CAN BE FOUND AT
WWW.DOROTAPERKINS.COM

Table of contents

What are feelings? 5

Examples of feelings 7

Is it ok to have feelings? 10

What does being mindful mean? 11

Examples of being mindful of your feelings 12

Identifying activities that cheer you up 15

Your own prescription for when you are feeling:

Sad 19

Bored 20

Missing someone 21

Nervous 22

A prescription for your own choice of feeling 23

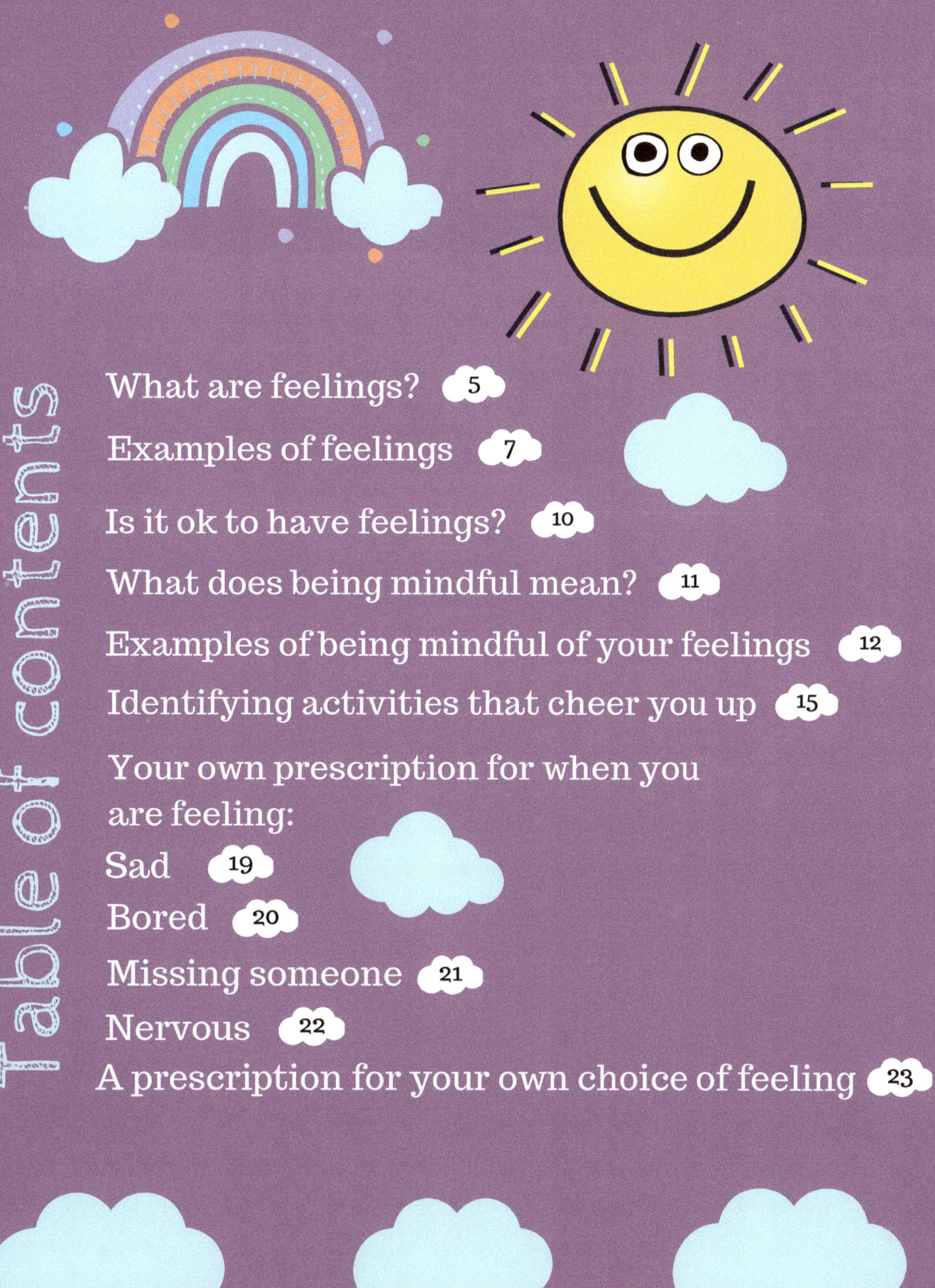

Table of contents

Mindful Activity 1 — 27
Mindful Activity 2 — 33
Mindful Activity 3 — 37
Mindful Activity 4 — 40
Mindful Activity 5 — 46

Reflection 1: Why is it good to be mindful? — 51

Reflection 2: How being mindful might help you. — 51

Notes — 52

<u>Additional mindful activities including:</u>
- calming strategies flashcards
- feelings flashcards

These can be downloaded for free from: www.dorotaperkins.com

Access password at the end of this book — 55

WHAT ARE FEELINGS ?

Feelings are your way of thinking and reacting to something that has happened to you.

For example, you may have received a birthday present and you know it's something you have really wanted for a long time. You may think: "Wow, this is great! I have always wanted this!" You may recognize this experience makes you happy and excited and you are smiling, maybe even wanting to jump from joy!

These positive reactions to your positive experience are called feelings. These types of feelings can be very special and can stay with you for a long time.

GIVE EXAMPLES OF YOUR FEELINGS WHEN YOU RECEIVED A PRESENT YOU WANTED:

To help you with some examples you can check page 7

WHAT ARE FEELINGS ?

Sometimes your reaction to something happening to you can be very different and less positive; sometimes your response can be negative. This is perfectly normal. Acknowledging all of your feelings is important.

For example, you may open your birthday present and you see it's something completely different from what you expected. You may think: "Oh... it's not what I thought it would be". You may recognize this makes you disappointed, a little bit sad, and maybe you even want to cry.

A good thing to do would be to talk to someone about how something made you feel. A lot of times there might be a positive way of solving your negative experience, and this is why it's important to talk to someone. It's not always easy to have these conversations about your feelings but it's very important to talk about them. Sharing your feelings can help you understand why you feel this way, and find ways to help you feel better.

Have a try of the activities in this book to help you understand and identify how different activities make you feel. This will help you to overcome the negative feelings you may experience.

EXAMPLES OF FEELINGS
CAN YOU ADD MORE?

- HAPPY
- SCARED
- BORED
- ....
- RELAXED
- ....
- SAD
- WORRIED
- CONFUSED
- LOVED
- GUILTY
- ....
- POSITIVE
- ANNOYED
- ....
- NERVOUS

EXAMPLE: THIS IS MINDFUL AMY WHO BAKED A CAKE BUT BURNT IT.

I FEEL A LITTLE BIT ANGRY

I FEEL SAD

I FEEL DISAPPOINTED

I FEEL TIRED

HOW CAN MINDFUL AMY MAKE HERSELF FEEL BETTER? "I WILL TRY TO BAKE A CAKE ANOTHER TIME. BUT FOR NOW, I WILL JUST GO TO PLAY WITH MY PET RABBIT BECAUSE HE MAKES ME SMILE EVERY TIME!"

EXAMPLE: THESE ARE MINDFUL FRIENDS ANDY & JAMAL WHO ARE WALKING RUFUS THE DOG.

I FEEL RELAXED

I FEEL GRATEFUL

I FEEL INTERESTED

I FEEL CHEERFUL

WHY DO MINDFUL FRIENDS ANDY & JAMAL WALK RUFUS? "WE LIKE SPENDING TIME TOGETHER BECAUSE WE ARE FRIENDS. WE TALK ABOUT RUFUS AND HIS FAVOURITE TREATS AND GAMES. IF WE ARE SAD OR BORED WE GO FOR A WALK OR PLAY IN THE GARDEN."

IS IT OK TO HAVE FEELINGS?

Feelings are a part of every human being. Even some animals have feelings too. You may feel different feelings from time to time: sometimes our feelings can be awesome but sometimes they are not so great. You might feel sad, scared, or angry and that is ok. You can feel many feelings at the same time, and that might be a little bit confusing, or you might even feel scared, but that is also normal and very human. The key to making this easier is to be aware of your feelings and try to name them. Talking to someone can help you to understand, name, and reflect on your feelings. Just remember that feeling all different types of feelings happens to everyone, and this is normal.

GIVE EXAMPLES OF YOUR FEELINGS WHEN YOU HAVEN'T FELT GREAT:

To help you with some examples you can check page 9

WHAT DOES BEING MINDFUL MEAN?

Being mindful means being aware of the moment you are in, often called the "present moment."

Being mindful also means that you are doing one thing at a time, rather than a million things together and getting overwhelmed!

Being in the present moment will help you to be aware of your thoughts, emotions, and feelings. In this book, you will learn about being mindful of your feelings.

Think about a time when you were colouring, painting, reading a book, or riding a bike. Do you remember how it made you feel?

If you were mindful, you might have noticed how these activities made you feel. You might have noticed you were: happy, sad, interested, bored, relaxed, or even angry. These are only a few examples of feelings, but there are so many more for you to explore! This workbook will help you to learn how different activities make you feel and what to do when you don't feel great. You will also learn which activities you can do to cheer yourself up.

EXAMPLE: THIS IS MINDFUL MIKE WHO IS RIDING HIS BIKE.

I FEEL HAPPY

I FEEL AWESOME

I FEEL EXCITED

I FEEL BRAVE

WHY DOES MINDFUL MIKE DO THIS ACTIVITY?
"I RIDE A BIKE BECAUSE IT MAKES ME FEEL SO GOOD! I WILL RIDE A BIKE WHEN I FEEL SAD OR BORED TOO, BECAUSE I KNOW IT WILL CHEER ME UP EVERY TIME!"

EXAMPLE: THIS IS MINDFUL MARK WHO LOST HIS COAT. HE WAS CERTAIN HE LEFT IT IN THE ROCKET.

I FEEL CONFUSED

I FEEL WORRIED

I FEEL UNSURE

WHAT CAN MINDFUL MARK DO?
HOW IS HE GOING TO FEEL BETTER?
"I FEEL ALL THESE DIFFERENT FEELINGS, BUT THAT IS OK. I NEED TO TALK TO MY OLDER SISTER; SHE ALWAYS MAKES ME HOT CHOCOLATE AND TALKS THINGS THROUGH."

EXAMPLE: THIS IS MINDFUL ZARA. SHE IS A SCOUT.

I FEEL EXCITED

I FEEL HAPPY

I FEEL AWESOME

I FEEL AMUSED

WHY DID MINDFUL ZARA JOIN THE SCOUTS?
"I JOINED THE SCOUTS BECAUSE IT MAKES ME FEEL GOOD ABOUT MYSELF! LAST TIME, I WAS PRACTISING COMPASS SKILLS. I FELT EXCITED ABOUT IT".

WRITE TWO ACTIVITIES THAT ALWAYS CHEER YOU UP

EXAMPLE: ......Drawing...... MAKES ME FEEL:

 Calm    Happy    Relaxed

.... MAKES ME FEEL:

EXAMPLE: THIS IS MINDFUL IMANI WHO LOVES SINGING.

I FEEL HAPPY

I FEEL AWESOME

I FEEL RELAXED

WHY DOES MINDFUL IMANI DO THIS ACTIVITY?
"I SING BECAUSE IT MAKES ME FEEL SO GOOD! I ALWAYS SING. SINGING GIVES ME MANY POSITIVE FEELINGS!"

WRITE MORE ACTIVITIES THAT ALWAYS CHEER YOU UP

.... MAKES ME FEEL:

.... MAKES ME FEEL:

WRITE ONE OCCASION WHEN YOU FELT NOT SO GREAT

EXAMPLE: I was missing my friend .... THIS MADE ME FEEL:

- Sad
- Annoyed
- Guilty

.... THIS MADE ME FEEL:

WHAT DID YOU DO TO FEEL BETTER? WHICH ACTIVITY CHEERED YOU UP?

....

IMAGINE YOU ARE A DOCTOR.
WRITE YOUR OWN PRESCRIPTION FOR WHEN YOU ARE FEELING SAD

Doctor's name _____

Date: _____

When I feel sad I can talk to:	When I feel sad I can try these activities:	Positive words or quotes to make me feel better:

Doctor's notes:

IMAGINE YOU ARE A DOCTOR. WRITE YOUR OWN PRESCRIPTION FOR WHEN YOU ARE FEELING BORED

Doctor's name _____

Date: _____

When I feel bored I can talk to:	When I feel bored I can try these activities:	Positive words or quotes to make me feel better:

Doctor's notes:

IMAGINE YOU ARE A DOCTOR.
WRITE YOUR OWN PRESCRIPTION FOR WHEN YOU ARE MISSING SOMEONE

Doctor's name _____

Date: _____

When I am missing someone I can talk to:	When I am missing someone I can try these activities:	Positive words or quotes to make me feel better:

Doctor's notes:

IMAGINE YOU ARE A DOCTOR.
WRITE YOUR OWN PRESCRIPTION FOR WHEN YOU ARE FEELING NERVOUS

Doctor's name _____

Date: _____

When I feel nervous I can talk to:	When I feel nervous I can try these activities:	Positive words or quotes to make me feel better:

Doctor's notes:

IMAGINE YOU ARE A DOCTOR.
WRITE YOUR OWN PRESCRIPTION FOR WHEN YOU ARE FEELING ....

Doctor's name _____

Date: _____

When I am .... I can talk to:	When I am.......................... I can try these activities:	Positive words or quotes to make me feel better:

Doctor's notes:

IMAGINE YOU ARE A DOCTOR.
WRITE YOUR OWN PRESCRIPTION FOR WHEN YOU ARE FEELING ....

Doctor's name _____

Date: _____

| When I am .... I can talk to: | When I am........................ I can try these activities: | Positive words or quotes to make me feel better: |

Doctor's notes:

IMAGINE YOU ARE A DOCTOR.
WRITE YOUR OWN PRESCRIPTION FOR WHEN YOU ARE FEELING ....

Doctor's name _____

Date: _____

When I am .... I can talk to:	When I am............................. I can try these activities:	Positive words or quotes to make me feel better:

Doctor's notes:

LET'S TRY SOME ACTIVITIES!

Mindful Activity 1

Colour this cute cat
and cut along the dotted line

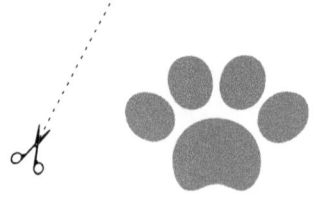

Mindful Activity 1

Colour this cute cat
and cut along the dotted line

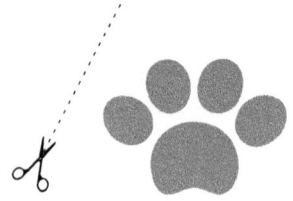

HOW DID ACTIVITY 1 MAKE YOU FEEL?

Circle your answer or write your own answer:

HAPPY

INTERESTED

SAD

CALM

SURPRISED

RELAXED

POSITIVE

ANGRY

INSPIRED

....

GOOD JOB!
NOW LET'S
TRY ANOTHER
ACTIVITY

Mindful Activity 2

♪♫

What song makes you happy? Why does this song make you happy? Write the lyrics for when you need cheering up.

_____
SONG TITLE

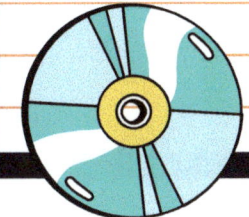

Mindful Activity 2

♫♪

List down words or sentences that give you positive feelings:

Example: I can do it!

1.
2.
3.
4.
5.
6.
7.
8.

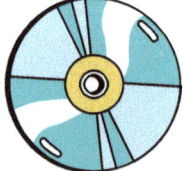

HOW DID ACTIVITY 2 MAKE YOU FEEL?

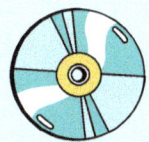

Circle your answer or write your own answer:

HAPPY   SAD
        INTERESTED
CALM   FRUSTRATED
        RELAXED
POSITIVE   CONFUSED
        ANGRY

....

GOOD JOB! CONTINUE BEING MINDFUL WITH THESE ACTIVITIES

Mindful Activity 3

Spend some time looking after your pet or playing with your pet. If you don't have a pet, draw some pictures of your favourite animals.

YOUR PET`S NAME

HOW DID ACTIVITY 3 MAKE YOU FEEL?

Circle your answer or write your own answer:

HAPPY   SAD

INTERESTED

CALM   FRUSTRATED

RELAXED

POSITIVE   CONFUSED

ANGRY

....

GOOD JOB!
NOW LET'S
TRY ANOTHER
ACTIVITY

Mindful Activity 4
veggie fun

Draw your favourite vegetable with eyes, eyebrows, and a mouth

POTATO

CARROT

LETTUCE

TOMATO

CORN

ONION

CAULIFLOWER

BROCCOLI

PEPPER

PUMPKIN

Mindful Activity 4
veggie fun

Draw your favourite vegetable with eyes, eyebrows, and a mouth

Mindful Activity 4

fruit fun

Draw your favourite fruit with eyes, eyebrows, and a mouth

APPLE

PEAR

GRAPE

STRAWBERRY

RASPBERRY

WATERMELON

ORANGE

CHERRY

BANANA

PINEAPPLE

Mindful Activity 4
fruit fun

Draw your favourite fruit with eyes, eyebrows, and a mouth

HOW DID ACTIVITY 4 MAKE YOU FEEL?

Circle your answer or write your own answer:

HAPPY

INTERESTED

CALM

RELAXED

POSITIVE

ANGRY

SAD

FRUSTRATED

CONFUSED

....

GOOD JOB! CONTINUE BEING MINDFUL WITH THESE ACTIVITIES

Mindful Activity 5

Colouring fun

Using the pages provided, write the first letter of your name in the middle. See the example on the next page.

Think of five objects beginning with the first letter of your name.

Draw these objects with a pencil.

Colour inside of your drawings using crayons.

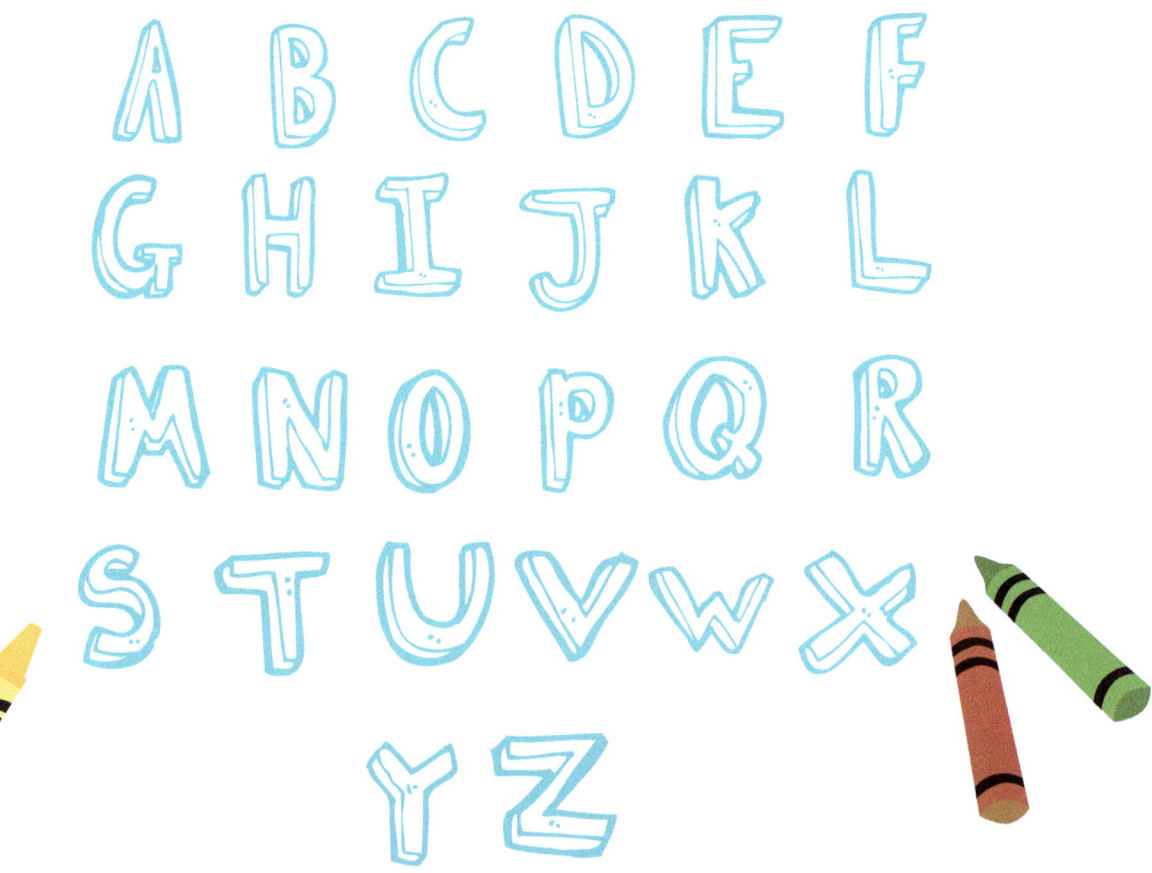

Mindful Activity 5
Example:

Mindful Activity 5
Colouring fun

HOW DID ACTIVITY 5 MAKE YOU FEEL?

Circle your answer or write your own answer:

HAPPY   SAD

　　INTERESTED

CALM   FRUSTRATED

　　RELAXED

　　　　　　CONFUSED

POSITIVE

　　ANGRY

....

GOOD JOB! CONTINUE BEING MINDFUL

HOW DO YOU FEEL AFTER DOING THE ACTIVITIES?

_____

_____

WHY DO YOU THINK IT IS GOOD TO BE MINDFUL?

_____

_____

HOW DO YOU THINK BEING MINDFUL MIGHT HELP YOU?

_____

_____

NOTES

NOTES

NOTES

FOR MORE RESOURCES

VISIT THE WEBSITE:
WWW.DOROTAPERKINS.COM

OR YOU CAN SIMPLY USE THIS QR CODE

Go to Free Download
Type access password: "mindful"

www.ingramcontent.com/pod-product-compliance
Lightning Source LLC
Chambersburg PA
CBHW041432040426
42450CB00022B/3473